WORLD CLASS CITIES

Singapore

Heather Kissock

AV2

www.av2books.com

Step 1
Go to **www.av2books.com**

Step 2
Enter this unique code

OTEVP4NMV

Step 3
Explore your interactive eBook!

AV2 is optimized for use on any device

Your interactive eBook comes with...

Contents
Browse a live contents page to easily navigate through resources

Audio
Listen to sections of the book read aloud

Videos
Watch informative video clips

Weblinks
Gain additional information for research

Try This!
Complete activities and hands-on experiments

Key Words
Study vocabulary, and complete a matching word activity

Quizzes
Test your knowledge

Slideshows
View images and captions

ISBN 978-1-7911-3306-1

Singapore

Contents

Get to Know Singapore

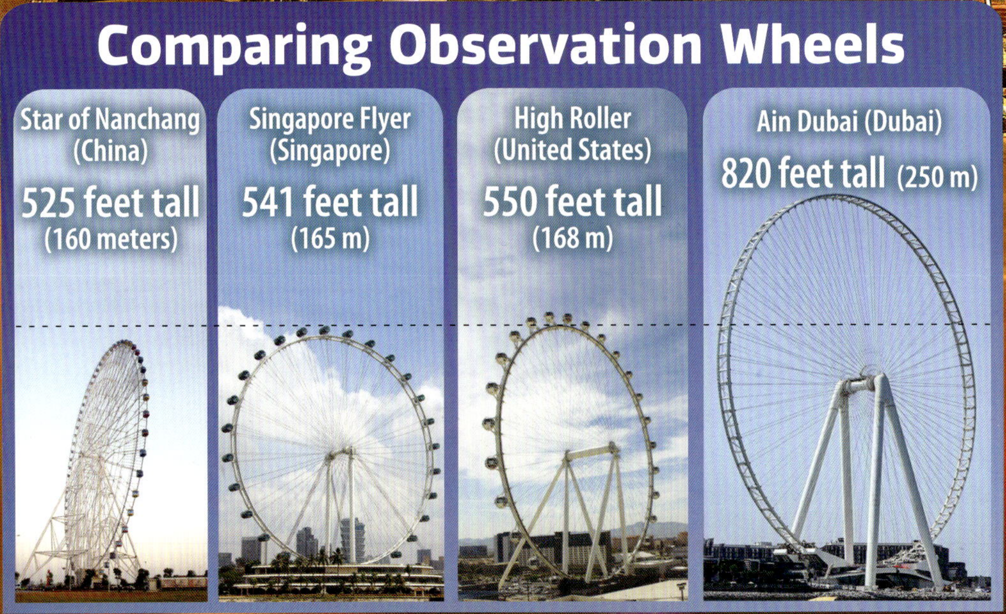

Singapore is both a city and a country. It is part of the **continent** of Asia. Singapore is home to the Singapore Flyer. This is one of the largest **observation** wheels in the world.

Where Is Singapore?

Singapore is made up of a main island and about 60 smaller islands. The main island sits off the southern tip of the Malay **Peninsula**. The country of Malaysia is north and east of Singapore. Indonesia's Riau Islands lie to Singapore's south.

Singapore offers visitors plenty to see and do. Most visitors take in the sights of the city's downtown. Many relax on the beaches along the coast. Others hop on a boat to tour the smaller islands.

Words to Know

Some people in Singapore speak Malay.
See if you can say a few words in this language.

Selamat pagi
Good morning

Terima kasih
Thank you

Selamat jalan
Goodbye

Ya
Yes

Tidak
No

Sama-sama
You're welcome

Climate

Singapore is in an area called the **tropics**. This means that the city stays warm all year. Thunderstorms are common. They bring heavy rains.

The city has two main seasons. They are based on winds called monsoons. The Northeast Monsoon lasts from December to March. It brings some of Singapore's rainiest days. The Southwest Monsoon takes place from June to September. It is slightly drier then.

A Year in Singapore

Southwest Monsoon Average Temperature
90° Fahrenheit (32° Celsius)

Northeast Monsoon Average Temperature
88° Fahrenheit (31° C)

Average Annual Rainfall
85 inches (2,159 millimeters)

DBS
HSBC

OCBC Bank

Population and Geography

Almost 6 million people live in Singapore. Most of them live on the city's main island. The city can seem quite crowded at times.

Singapore was built along the Singapore River. This river flows through the heart of the city. It is about 2 miles (3.2 kilometers) long.

Singapore Population by Age

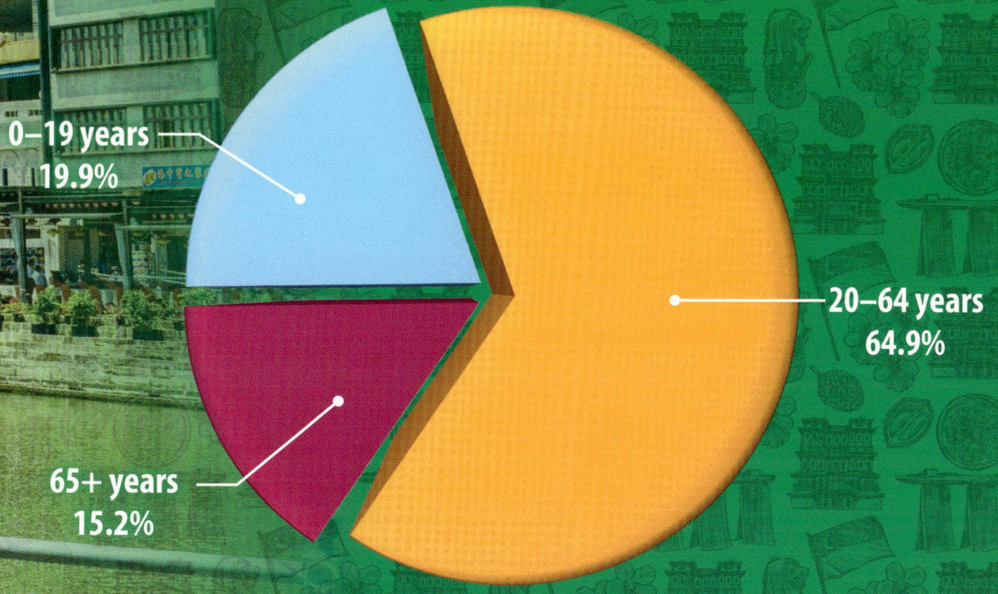

Beginnings

The Malay People were living in Singapore long before anyone else. They have been there for at least 700 years. Europeans began to explore the area in the 1400s. In 1824, the British took control of Singapore.

Singapore grew in size under the British. It became an important **port** city for Asia. In 1963, Singapore declared its **independence** from Great Britain. It became a nation in its own right two years later.

Singapore Timeline

Singapore has been the site of many important events over the years. All have made the city what it is today.

1298 AD

Singapore's first settlements are established.

1400s

Europeans begin to explore Southeast Asia.

1819

A British man named Stamford Raffles sets up a trading post in Singapore.

1824

The British take control of Singapore. It later becomes a British **colony**.

1965

Singapore becomes an independent nation.

2019

Singapore marks the 200th anniversary of its founding by Stamford Raffles.

Tourism

Gardens by the Bay is one of the most visited tourist sites in Singapore. It is made up of three different gardens. One of these, the Supertree Grove, has giant trees made of steel and concrete.

The National Museum of Singapore is the city's largest museum. People come here to learn about Singapore's past. They can also see how the city has changed over time.

Things to Do in Singapore

Merlion Fountain

Tourists often head to the waterfront to see the Merlion Fountain. The merlion is a **mythical** creature. It is part lion and part fish.

ArtScience Museum

The outside of this museum is shaped like a **lotus** blossom. Inside are displays that combine art and science.

Buddha Tooth Relic Temple
This is Singapore's best-known **Buddhist** temple. Besides being a place of **worship**, it also serves as a meeting place and museum.

Helix Bridge
This bridge crosses the Singapore River. It provides visitors with great views of the city's **skyline**.

Singapore Zoo
One of the best times to visit this zoo is at night. Its Night Safari lets visitors see how animals behave after dark.

Gold Coast
2018
STIGA
STIGA
CGF
Gold Coast 20
Gold Coast 2018
红双喜
DHS

Sports

Soccer is Singapore's most popular **spectator sport**. The city has nine main teams. Singapore's national team is one of the best in Southeast Asia.

Singapore is also known for its table tennis players. These athletes compete around the world. They have won medals at the Olympics and other major sporting events.

Economy

Singapore has one of the world's largest ports. Huge ships arrive and leave from there every day. These ships carry goods to all parts of the world.

Many goods are also made in Singapore. This makes the city a center for **manufacturing**. Some of the key items made in Singapore are plastics and batteries.

Singapore's Top 3 Industries

1. Manufacturing
2. Wholesale and Retail Trade
3. Business Services

ANTOINE DE SAINT EXUPERY

Quiz

1 To which continent does Singapore belong?

ANSWER: Asia

2 How many main seasons does Singapore have?

ANSWER: Two

3 How many people live in Singapore?

ANSWER: Almost 6 million

4 In what year did Singapore become a nation in its own right?

ANSWER: 1965

5 Which tourist site is home to the Supertree Grove?

ANSWER: Gardens by the Bay

6 What is a merlion?

ANSWER: A mythical creature that is part lion and part fish

7 What is Singapore's most popular spectator sport?

ANSWER: Soccer

8 What is Singapore's top industry?

ANSWER: Manufacturing

Key Words

Buddhist: someone who follows the teachings of a man called Buddha

colony: a territory ruled by another country

continent: one of seven large land areas on Earth

independence: freedom from the control of others

lotus: a plant with large pink, white, or yellow flowers

manufacturing: making something with the use of machinery

mythical: imaginary, not real

observation: the act of watching something

peninsula: a piece of land that sticks out into water from a larger body of land

port: a place where ships can dock safely

reserve: land used for a special purpose

skyline: the outline of buildings seen against the sky

spectator sport: a sport that people go to watch

temples: buildings that are used for worship

tropics: a region of Earth that is near the equator

worship: honor a god

Index

Published by AV2
276 5th Avenue, Suite 704 #917
New York, NY 10001
Website: www.av2books.com

Library of Congress Cataloging-in-Publication Data
Names: Kissock, Heather, author.
Title: Singapore / Heather Kissock.
Description: New York, NY : AV2, [2022] | Series: World class cities | Includes index. | Audience: Ages 8-11 | Audience: Grades 2-3
Identifiers: LCCN 2021003472 (print) | LCCN 2021003473 (ebook) | ISBN 9781791138394 (library binding) | ISBN 9781791138400 (paperback) | ISBN 9781791138417
Subjects: LCSH: Singapore--Juvenile literature.
Classification: LCC DS609 .K57 2022 (print) | LCC DS609 (ebook) | DDC 959.57--dc23
LC record available at https://lccn.loc.gov/2021003472
LC ebook record available at https://lccn.loc.gov/2021003473

Printed in Guangzhou, China
1 2 3 4 5 6 7 8 9 0 25 24 23 22 21

022021
101120

Project Coordinator: Heather Kissock
Designer: Ana María Vidal

Every reasonable effort has been made to trace ownership and to obtain permission to reprint copyright material. The publishers would be pleased to have any errors or omissions brought to their attention so that they may be corrected in subsequent printings.

AV2 acknowledges Getty Images, Alamy, Newscom, Bridgeman Images, and Dreamstime as its primary image suppliers for this title.